ATTACK OF THE 50 FOOT MIKHAELA: Cartoons by Mikhaela Reid
First printing, 2007

Published by Calamity Press, Lowell, Mass.

Read Mikhaela Reid's cartoons and blog online at **www.mikhaela.net**
E-mail Mikhaela Reid at **toons@mikhaela.net**

Book design and cover by Mikhaela Reid.

THANKS TO: Beryl Reid, Paul Katler, Max Katler and Sylvia Katler; Gail Wood; Ted Rall; Keith Knight, Alison Bechdel and Howard Cruse; Cartoonists With Attitude; Susan Ryan-Vollmar; Sean Bieri; Polly Davis-Doig; Jessica Valenti, Feministing and The Real Hot 100; Clay Bennett and Cindy Procious; Jaclyn Friedman and the Center for New Words; Márta Fodor, Stephanie Bencin, Mary Vonckx, Laleña Ga rcia and Jon Goldberg; Marlo Pedroso; Geoffrey Fowler; Warren Bernard; and many other fine people who bear no resemblance to Dick Cheney.

Attack OF THE 50 FT. MIKHAELA

Cartoons by

MIKHAELA REID

Foreword by
TED RALL

CALAMITY PRESS · Lowell, Massachusetts

FOR MASHEKA

CONTENTS

FOREWORD
BY TED RALL

DURING THE MID-1980S, while Reagan-era Americans were donning frilly miniskirts and twisting the night away to Dire Straights, Frankie Goes to Hollywood and side two of Flipper's "Generic" LP, Zhang Juzhong was sifting through Grave M344 at the Jiahu archeological dig in China's Henan Province. One afternoon in May 1987, after four years, he noticed a stash of tortoise shells. One shell in particular drew his attention.

"It felt so smooth," he remembers. "Its owners must have often held it in their hands." On the plastron (underside) of the shell was an eye-shaped sign, which resembled a pictograph for "eye" in later so-called oracle bones. The 8,600-year-old carving, which may represent the earliest known example of human writing, predates writing discovered in Mesopotamia by 2,000 years. Said Zhang: "We were exhilarated, and bought meat and liquor for celebration."

Attack of the 50-Foot Mikhaela, the book you hold in your hands, is an even more valuable find than Zhang's.

Unlike Zhang's tortoise shell, Mikhaela Reid's political cartoons offer both words and text in an easy-to-digest "cartoon" format. Moreover, they deliver trenchant political commentary about the United States of America, its leaders and citizenry near the end of its remarkable 231-year run. Can some old tortoise shell say that?

It cannot.

Mikhaela's cartoons, moreover, have only been in print for six years. They represent a commodity far rarer and more rarified than tortoises, which have been around for 300 million years and have arguably overstayed their welcome.

Any loser can dig in a hole. Braving the crowds at a convention of comics fans, on the other hand, requires perseverance, bravado and good taste—taste that you've proven merely by reading these words. Oh, and tolerance. Lots and lots of tolerance.

Where else but Mikhaela's cartoons will you find such a delicious blend of vicious political satire, pop culture commentary and terrifying depictions of even more terrifying public officials? Not in most newspapers—and certainly not on some tortoise shell.

Before parting, I feel it my duty to address the packaging of this tome and specifically its title. Is Mikhaela 50 feet tall, you ask?

Answer: Not metaphorically. Physically, however, yes—yes, she is. And she would very much appreciate it if you would write to the owners of local businesses to ask them to please, pretty please, increase their ceiling heights for her convenience.

And also: Is this book literally an "attack"?

And the answer is again yes...yes it is. It is an attack on stupidity, on self-righteousness, on selfishness, on bigotry, on pomposity, and on generalized idiocy. As such it deserves to outlast every example of literature and art that humanity has produced since that Ancient Someone scratched that pictograph in what is today central China, as well as everything to follow for another 8,200 years.

Purchase this book (don't ask the price—just hand over your wallet), and you will not only immortalize yourself—you will become entitled to celebrate your life with a meal of meat and/or liquor.

Ted Rall draws cartoons, writes columns and puts out books. His latest books are his graphic travelogue about Central Asia, Silk Road to Ruin, *and a collection of cartoons,* America Gone Wild.

INTRODUCTION

BY MIKHAELA REID

THE YEAR WAS 1983, but I remember it like it was yesterday. Terrified by Reagan's pompadour on our tiny black-and-white TV, I toddled into the kitchen at top speed and tugged at my mother's jeans:

"Mommy," I announced, "when I grow up, I want to get paid very little money to draw mean pictures and get nasty e-mails from rightwing nutjobs."

Actually, until I was fourteen, my ambition was to be a science fiction novelist. I consumed a steady diet of dystopia, wrote short stories about apocalyptic gold-plated space viruses and pictured myself surrounded by adoring fans, each clutching a copy of my latest bleak bestseller.

But I was always a political girl—in a family like mine, anything less would have been an assault on family values. My brother and I could never get enough of our parents' 1970s-tastic stories about leading high school walkouts, marching for gay power and getting tear-gassed at anti-Vietnam War actions. The Civil Rights Movement documentary series *Eyes on the Prize* was required annual family viewing.

At age seven, I joined the picket lines with my father for a teacher's strike, waving a sign from atop his shoulders. When I was nine, I patiently explained to an irate substitute teacher that I had a different last name than Daddy because Mommy was a feminist. When I was fourteen my Zadie (grandfather) Leon gave me a pile of *Nation* and *In These Times* back issues and bought me a subscription to *Liberal Opinion*. He advised me to pay close attention to the cartoons.

Pay attention I did, attacking each issue with scissors to extract my favorite Molly Ivins columns and Tom Tomorrow and Tom Toles cartoons. Meanwhile I had discovered political punk rock and Ted Rall's angry social commentary cartoons, as well as riot grrrl music and my all-time-favorite comic strip, Alison Bechdel's political lesbian soap opera, *Dykes to Watch Out For*.

My first political cartoon for the 1996 Lowell High School *Review* skewered the school dress code (see "Part 3: The Early Years"); the second was a pen-and-ink retaliation against the bullies who harassed members of our Gay/Straight Alliance. I got an overwhelming response, and I was almost hooked.

But in the end it was George W. Bush who rescued me from the dreary life of a non-cartoonist. In the fall of 2001, I was happily enthralled by my studies in anthropology and photography at Harvard, dissecting cultural narratives and debating post-modern aesthetics.

Then some asshole extremists killed 3,000 innocent Americans. And our Election-Stealer-in-Chief took that as an opportunity to gut social spending, detain and deport innocent immigrants, bomb the crap out of Afghanistan and Iraq, set up an island torture camp and insert a camera into every American colon.

I wasn't just angry, I was **ANGRY** on a large—you might say 50-foot—scale. Smalltime arguments with fellow students over the Patriot Act were no longer enough. I applied for an editorial cartoonist slot in *The Harvard Crimson* (and later, *The Boston Phoenix*). And thus my weekly strip, "The Boiling Point," was born.

I haven't stopped drawing—or fuming—since. I hope the next election will bring a reasonably less evil leader so I can relax and write more jokes about relationships and fashion, but I'm not holding my breath.

Take one set left-wing parents, two parts punk rock—a little Dead Kennedys here, a little Bikini Kill there—one part Orwell, Vonnegut, Twain and Butler (Octavia, that is). Add one stolen election, one inarticulate, smirking, trigger-happy madman, two illegal wars, one widening income gap, one crumbling education system and one fundamentalist movement bent on a chastity belt for every woman, shock therapy for every gay person and Bible stories in every science textbook. Shake vigorously, and serve weekly.

The cartoons in this book represent the best results of that recipe, in my opinion or that of the readers whose kind comments have kept me drawing these past six years. Some strips are are sarcastic, some are silly, and some are so angry they even make *me* wince. Zadie would be proud.

Mikhaela B. Reid, April 2007

Sometimes people want to know

Where I Get it From

in other words: how did I get so... political?

I definitely get a healthy dose of ~~paranoia~~ ~~cynicism~~ realism from my dad.

Hey, thanks a lot for putting me in this cartoon. Now Ashcroft will tap my phone too!

My Government Took Away My Civil Liberties And All I Got Was This Lousy T-Shirt

And then there's his dad, my Zadie Katler, who bought me lots of lefty magazines when I was a kid. His favorite part was the political cartoons...

Now, Mikhaela, I hope you and your friends are marching for homosexual rights!

And of course my mom's dad, Granddaddy Reid, who took me for motorcycle rides when I was three...

★!✪?⧆! Reagan @⧆!#!!

Zadie and Granddaddy would have a lot to say about the current political situation if they were still around...

Goddamned piece of $#!@ cutting vets' benefits @!✱ @!#⧆!!

Oh boy, two empty trailers, now that's proof of Iraq's WMD's...

But they're not, so it's up to me to carry on the tradition. So this one's for my granddads...

STOP BUSH

In Loving Memory of Leon Katler 1919–1998 Gordon Reid 1930–1983

My dad gets lots of compliments on that T-shirt when he wears it around Brooklyn.

PART 1
THE BOILING POINT

It's what warmongers crave!

Bush vs. My Cat!

A completely pointless battle of wits or the lack thereof

★ extremely limited vocabulary

★ complete lack of vocabulary

★ chokes on pretzels, foreign policy

★ chokes on electrical cords, rubber bands

★ Lazy, often on vacation

★ Lazy, always on vacation

★ attacks preemptively, never apologizes

★ attacks preemptively, never apologizes

★ makes whole country pay for giant illegal war messes

★ makes me clean up piles of half-digested hair and shoelaces

George W. Bush: slightly less stupid and lazy than my cat.   Happy April!

Before I get any more angry letters about this one: it was an APRIL FOOL'S JOKE, people.
Obviously my cat would make the better President.

Haggard led a 30-million strong anti-gay evangelical group until it came out that he had been buying sex and meth from a male massage therapist for three years. James Dobson supervised his remarkably rapid "cure."

Some folks criticize Congress for extending tax cuts while slashing social programs. But they always forget to mention

How tax cuts for the rich can help YOU!

Tax cut bills make an excellent source of heat when you've been kicked off welfare!

Don't worry about Medicare cuts. Just bandage your wounds with tax break legislation!

Education, schmeducation! With reduced student loans, you couldn't have sent them to college anyway!

Who needs food stamps when you have tax cut salad?

A rising tide lifts all yachts.

the brighter side of... A Bush Supreme Court

Newer, better excuse for not being in the mood

Long lines at the voting booth, voting, finally abolished

Death penalty for non-Christians makes it way easier to find an apartment

That coat-hanger-company stock you bought is totally going to outperform Google

The Bushies plan to rebuild the Gulf Coast by ignoring prevailing wage laws and environmental regulations. Why not just go all the way and...

Let Them Eat Toxic Sludge

Barbara Bush on Katrina evacuees living in Houston's Astrodome: "So many of the people in the arena here, you know, were underprivileged anyway, so this—this (she chuckles slightly) is working very well for them."

Americans brag about their
Gold Plated Health Plans

Our awesome plan paid for so much of my cancer care, we nearly avoided bankruptcy!

My ER visit only cost me TWO months rent—who's laughing now, Canada?

Your mama's copays are so high, she had to marry me for my prescription drug coverage!

I could get my clap cured by any one of the FIVE doctors in my plan network.

Bush claims the biggest problem with American health insurance is that it's too darn comprehensive and fancy and affordable and encrusted with big sparkly diamonds.

President Giuliani

The Early Years

2009: Clean Up America Act

Sends all peep-show operators, homeless people, welfare recipients, art-museum curators to labor camp on Mars.

2010: Racial Profiling Flap

Giuliani-led military accidentally drops 41 nukes on Africa, claims to have mistaken continent's wallet for a gun.

Hey, this continent was no choir boy— it probably had a criminal record!

K FIX NEWS

RUDY: TRAGEDY "COULDN'T BE HELPED"

RACE-BAITER SHARPTON BLAMES BRAVE TROOPS

2011: Sexy Cabinetgate

Scandal finally sticks when "Randy Rudy" caught in bed with entire advisory staff; approval rating plummets to 12%.

Oct. 2012: Tragedy Strikes

Half of U.S. submerged in deadly global-warming accident; a shaken yet defiant Giuliani shows emotion, vows to rebuild.

Nov. 2012:

All scandals forgotten, Giuliani elected Intergalatic Hero-President-For-Life.

HERO OF THE MILLENIUM

TIME

Africa who?

Don't even get me started on this guy.

Personal Economic Indicators

The I'll-Be-Feeding-My-Kids-Ramen-Noodles-Again-Tonight Consumption Composite

The Oh-God-I-Just-Know-I'm-Going-To-Get-Downsized-Next-Week Futures Index

The No-Insurance-and--Medical-Bills-So-High-I'm-Getting-Sicker-Just-Worrying-About-Trying-to-Pay-Them Weighted Average

The Super-Excited-About-Bush's-Plan-to-Privatize-Social-Security Index

For three years I worked as an information graphics designer at *The Wall Street Journal*, charting indicators like the Consumer Confidence Index and the Dow Jones Industrial Average.

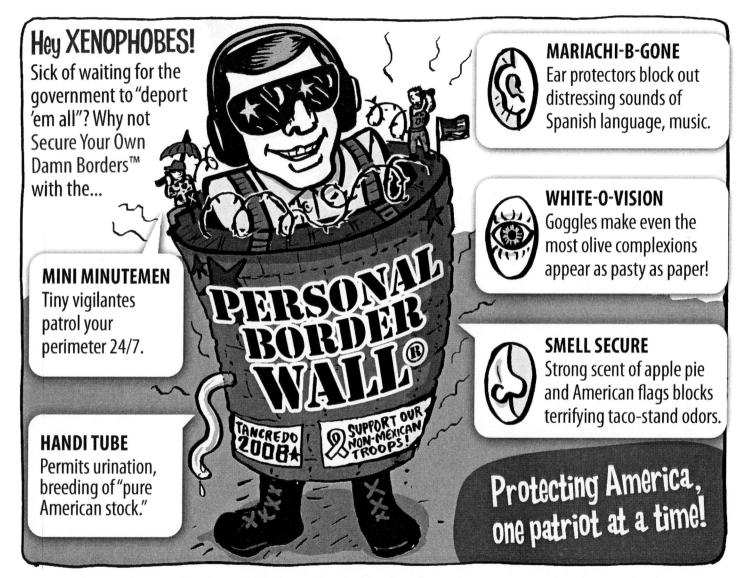

One reader was deeply—DEEPLY!—offended by the phrase "pasty as paper," and wanted to know why I had such a grudge against white people.

BITTER PILL

"You know the feeling. The economy is slumping, your polls are slipping and Osama is still missing..."

"But thanks to the biggest breakthrough since Botox, you don't have to let that cramp your lifestyle!"

"Introducing BombIraq®, the all-in-one patriotism and popularity booster. Ask your doctor about BombIraq® today..."

"(Common side effects include, but are not limited to: increased bloating of the military budget, slashed social spending, worldwide hatred and disgust, massive civilian casualties and/or biological/nuclear catastrophes. Do not take BombIraq® if you are pregnant, nursing, or in possession of more than two brain cells.)"

by mikhaela '02

The maiden voyage of "The Boiling Point": my first cartoon for *The Boston Phoenix* while I was still a senior at Harvard. The day it was published I took a ride on the T, picked up an abandoned *Phoenix* and discovered my cartoon had been carefully clipped out. Wow.

the brighter side of Long-Term Unemployment!

**At long last, you have time to...
Experiment with your cooking!**

Do a little redecorating!

Get in touch with old friends!

**And last, but not least...
Catch up on the news!**

Bride vs. Bride

Same-sex marriage edition!

Honey, I can't decide—should our place cards be on lilac paper with lavender ribbons, or lavender paper with lilac ribbons?

OK, Bridezilla, what gives? One minute you're fighting poverty, AIDS, and racism, and the next all you care about is cards, cakes and catering.

Where's the activist I fell in love with?

I'm still an activist, I'm just fighting the conservatives who'd rather see us in shock treatments than wedding gowns.

So those overpriced cases of champagne you ordered are actually part of your complex and multi-faceted marriage-equality strategy?

Be that way. I'll just have to keep the heart-shaped waffle iron Great-Aunt Gladys just bought us all for myself!

Marriage equality is crucial. But too often other critical lesbian/gay/bisexual/transgender issues get obscured by all that wedding cake.

WHAT TO EXPECT WHEN YOU'RE PRE-EXPECTING!

Reassuring advice for today's potential fetus incubator!

SIGNS OF PRE-PREGNANCY

Are you a menstruating female between puberty and "the change"? Do Republicans restrict your access to birth control and family planning? Congratulations! You're pre-pregnant!

PRE-PREGNANCY + TESTS -

Do you ever do anything that could potentially harm a pre-child, such as drinking, jogging, eating spicy fish, working outside the home or lacking moral values? Pre-pregnancy experts advise that you should be incarcerated—for the pre-baby's sake!

WHAT NOT TO EXPECT

Social services for any existing children, access to low-cost health care, sympathy, respect, people giving up their seats on the subway.

Did you know?
It's not YOUR health that matters—it's that of the womb that could bear an unborn child!

My take on federal guidelines that treated all women from menstruation to menopause as "pre-pregnant" got reprinted in *The Guardian* (UK). Feministing.com Executive Editor Jessica Valenti bought the original.

TEACHING (IN)TOLERANCE!

Anti-gay groups successfully sued a Maryland school board for not teaching students that homosexuality is a "treatable disease." But that's not the only view unfairly excluded from public classrooms!

After six exciting weeks at reparative therapy camp, little Jimmy killed himself, saving his parents from the shame of having a gay son!

You do realize that you Jews are going to burn in the fires of hell for all eternity, don't you?

Now, who remembers why the fairer sex is genetically incapable of scientific thought?

Today Imperial Wizard Bob is going to teach us that we're stupid little monkeys who should go back to Africa!

Now that's what I call "diversity of opinion."

So I'm standing in a crowd of 10,000 gorgeous sweaty men wearing nothing but sunglasses and combat boots—and we've all got universal health care and a living wage.

Rick Santorum, James Dobson and Mitt Romney come out as flaming queens and start a pro-choice feminist anti-tax-cut anti-death-penalty drag revue.

So the hot UPS girl comes to your desk in her little brown shorts...

And as you sign for your package, you realize you're as well-respected and well-paid as the men in your office who do the same job.

Dick Cheney... in handcuffs.

I was shocked when this got reprinted in the *Los Angeles Times*—I never expected my first cartoon in a mainstream daily newspaper to feature a naked male couple in bed talking about their fantasies.

Christian conservatives are up in arms over the insidious messages of "tolerance" and "diversity" promoted by SpongeBob SquarePants. But with a few small modifications, even Mr. FancyPants could be a healthy role model. Presenting:

BrickBob GAYBASH!

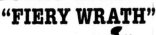

IN WACKY EPISODES LIKE:

"THE GOOD PLAGUE"

BrickBob teaches the kiddies that AIDS is God's revenge on sodomites and feminists.

"FIERY WRATH"

BrickBob wields his 2 x 4 of Justice on Muppet sissies like Bert and Ernie.

"HATE IS GREAT"

BrickBob and his hunting buddy attend a Ku Klux Klan rally.

"FAMILY VALUES"

When BrickBob discovers his daughter is a lesbo, will he beat her, throw her out on the street, or send her to shock therapy? Stay tuned!

Remember, kids: Being yourself... is a sin!

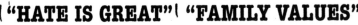

A reader took this cartoon literally and cussed me out for my gay-bashing. Maybe it *was* too close to the truth: two weeks after I drew this came the news that Alan Keyes had kicked out his teenage lesbian daughter.

Breakup Lines

for the Bush era

Hey, don't whine to me—I've designated the porch as a free speech zone.

Think of this as a preemptive strike—I have to break up with you NOW before I stop loving you LATER.

It's not just me, sweetheart—the coalition agrees it's time for both of us to move on.

I've got some really reliable intelligence that says we should just be friends.

But I'm not DUMPING you, baby —I'm SPREADING LIBERTY!

mikhaela reid 2005 ★ www.mikhaela.net ★ toons@mikhaela.net

Don't tell me you've never used one of these!

YOUR ★ YUCKY ♥ BODY ★

a repair manual

Your **right ear** is slightly too big. No one will ever love you.

Embrace diversity! Women of every shape, age and color can become marginally less ugly if they spend lots of money!

SEXY SURGERY SPOTLIGHT!

Love your body tip! True beauty lies within a really bony ribcage that hasn't seen any food but watery salt-free cabbage soup.

That **weird little bump** on your thigh bone is a big DON'T this season. Have you considered amputation?

TOE BYPASS
What could be more *slimming* and *feminine* than permanent pointy heels?

You don't have to be a size 0 to be pretty! Size 4 is also permissible—if you're super-tall!

BELLY-DECTOMY
Let's face it, ladies: liposuction and stomach stapling don't get at the real problem: even the flattest tummy is just *inherently icky!*

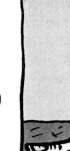

I freely admit to being a women's magazine junkie. The toe thing is quasi-real—a significant number of women pay to have their toes reshaped or removed, the better to fit into high-end high heels.

34

Sick of your kids being exposed to filth like *Will and Grace*? Thank God for

SANTORUM KNOWS BEST

The wit and wisdom of the senator from Pennsylvania on your very own TV!

Old School, Home School

But girls, if we didn't homeschool you, you'd be brainwashed by radical feminists into wanting a career!

Geography Lessons

Jesus told me that evil liberal gamma zeltron rays emanating from Boston cause priests to molest altar boys!

Birds + (Heterosexual) Bees

Kids, your mother and I are about to have old-fashioned man-on-woman sex—as opposed to man-on-man or man-on-dog sex!

Work and Play

Son, someday you may learn your top aide is a filthy negro sodomite—but that's OK as long as he gets you elected!

Tune in next week for more life lessons from America's wisest dad!

True fact: Santorum blamed the priest abuse scandal on Boston's liberalism, and his top aide was a gay black man.

My first Hurricane Katrina cartoon reaction.

36

We must protect pharmacists' rights to Not Do Their Damn Jobs and Make Women Feel Like Crap!

Confessions of a Closet Conservationist!

"It's not easy being a secret... TREE HUGGER!"

By day I talk the talk, but inside, I'm a man torn apart by twisted urges!

Senator, EVERYONE knows global warming is a myth cooked up by hairy-legged hippie terrorists!

Does he know I buy carbon offsets?

I knew I'd hit the bottom of the recycling bin when I awoke one night to find myself giving my annual bonus to save owls, whales, panda bears—and CARIBOU.

"Stop the drilling in the Arct"—oh no!

My cover is starting to crack. Yesterday my wife caught me in a compromising position with a compact fluorescent bulb...

This isn't what it looks like!

And today I found myself fondling the thermostat again!

I'm an oil lobbyist, for Chrissakes! What would my boss say if he found my stash of canvas shopping bags?

Thank God nothing I've done in my twilight life, however emboldening to the enemies of American free enterprise....

Could even begin to offset the ass-pounding I've given this planet!

"Gay MARRIAGE Drove Us to DIVORCE!"

- Not convinced old-fashioned marriage needs protecting? Then take heed, dear reader, as hapless heterosexuals tell the **SHOCKING** **TRUE TALES** of how homosexuals harmed their once-happy unions!

mikhaela '04 ★ www.mikhaela.net

"She wanted a May wedding—but the chapel was booked... by lesbians!"

"We keep fighting over which is more disgusting—dyke weddings, or fag weddings?"

"Agnes wakes me up every goddamn second shrieking 'We're going to go EXTINCT!'"

"The thought of homos filing joint tax returns, visiting each other in hospitals, and getting health care and Social Security benefits is driving me to drink."

"My husband met a younger woman—at a Defense of Marriage rally!"

The conservative claim that marriage equality would destroy existing marriages has always puzzled me.

The Super-Duper Quick + Easy Guide to

Not Becoming a Terror Suspect

These simple steps are so straightforward that you deserve to be shot if you can't follow them!

DON'T wear a backpack or a puffy jacket!

DON'T be an electrician.

DON'T be a Muslim, talk to Muslims, walk next to a Muslim or live in the same building as Muslims!

DON'T be black or brown! Excessive tanning is also inadvisable.

DON'T run away from large gangs of armed men in ordinary clothes!

DO realize that if that gang (of plainclothes police) chases you into the subway, pushes you to the ground and shoots you seven times in the head, officials will say your death was "tragic," but necessary.

Jean Charles de Menezes was a legal Brazilian immigrant to the U.K., an electrician who had the misfortune to be living in the same block as the suspected London subway bombers. The police claimed their actions were justified due to his "suspiciously warm" clothing, brown complexion and electrician's tool set.

Abstinence Education

Bush left thousands of poor black people to die in New Orleans while he played guitar and ate cake. People are dying every day in Iraq because of his lies. He wants to amend the goddamn Constitution to keep us from getting married...

Not that I'd WANT to marry you after what you did.

Baby, how many times do I have to say it? I'm REALLY sorry I voted for that jerk. But how long are you going to make me sleep on this couch?

-kiss-

Until Karl Rove goes to jail and Dick Cheney gets indicted.

Sweet dreams!

mikhaela '05 ★ www.mikhaela.net ★ toons@mikhaela.net

There once was a time, a beautiful, happy, carefree time, when we dared to hope that the CIA Leak Scandal would be Dick Cheney's undoing. I guess this poor woman is still sleeping on the couch.

stop republican adoption!

(Cartoon inspired by an actual Republican adoption ban bill submitted in protest by Ohio State Senator Robert Hagan)

They recruit!

43

FAILED RECRUITING SLOGANS

Ask Ann Coulter

STRAIGHT TALK FROM MS. RIGHT!

Q. Dear Ann,
My future mother-in-law refuses to attend my wedding unless I wear her ugly old dress.
What should I do?
—*Frazzled in Flint*

A. Dear Frazzled,
Like all godless liberals, you deserve to know what it is like to be eviscerated with a dull spoon as your tongue is wound around the spines of a poison caterpillar.
—*Sincerely,*
Ann

Q. Dear Ann,
What would be the most appropriate thing to wear to a summer cocktail party in the Hamptons?
—*Nervous in NYC*

A. Dear Nervous,
Your armpits have the stench of 1,000 Muslim terrorists.
Women should never have been given the vote.
—*Yours, Ann*

SHAPELY WISDOM FROM A CONSERVATIVE BEAUTY!

The college conservative group Young America's Foundation sold an Ann Coulter "pinup" poster as a fundraiser: "The Beauty of Conservatism. Ann Coulter... proves it is possible to be beautiful, intelligent and conservative."

FIGHTIN' BILL O'REILLY AND HIS ELVES OF FURY BRING THE HORROR IN...

A Christmas BATTLE!

Eat my tinsel, secular scum!

ONE DAY AT ~~FOX~~ THE NORTH POLE...

Well, we tore down that mall's "Happy Holidays" banner in the nick of time—but what's this?! A school without a Christmas pageant?!

To the war sleigh!

SCOUTING OUT THE SCENE...

It's far worse than I feared-not a nativity scene in sight. This one's for the manger, boys!

FACE-TO-FACE WITH THE ENEMY!

Hands up, pipsqueaks! Gimme some real Christian carols!

And none of that dreidel dreidel Kwaanza bells crap!

But this is a public school—we have children of many faiths here!

Silence, ACLU-loving witch!

If you don't want to live in a Christian country, you and your menorah-sucking friends can move to Iraq!

SWEET VICTORY!

Peace on Earth and goodwill towards men, motherf**kers!!!

Oh, Bill O'Reilly, why must you hit me in the face with your righteous Christmas gun?

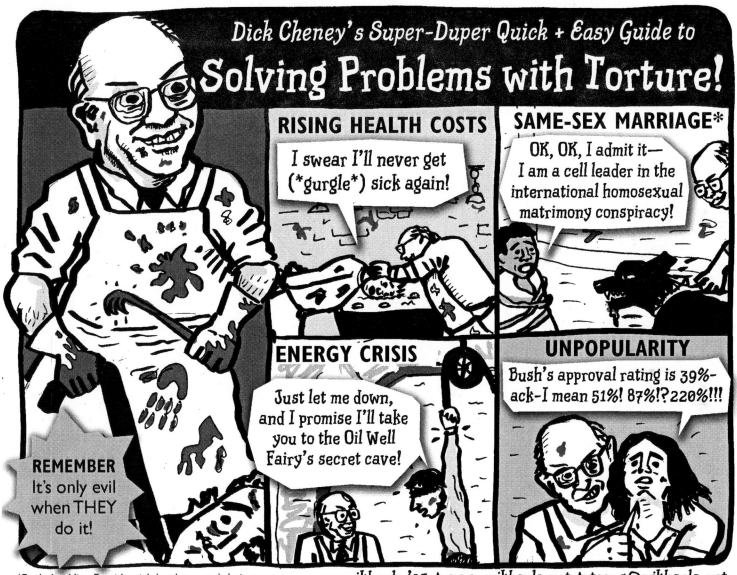

In addition to my regular weekly strip "The Boiling Point," I draw New-York themed cartoons for a community newspaper in Manhattan, *Chelsea Now*. This one is a little shoutout to my own political crafting group. In case you can't tell, the undercover policeman is knitting handcuffs and a nightstick.

when **will** **it** **stop?**

www.mikhaela.net

MIKHAELA 2006

Amadou Diallo
41 shots, 1999

Patrick Dorismond
1999

Timothy Stansbury
2004

Sean Bell
50 shots, 2006

In November 2006, five policemen fired a total of 50 shots at three innocent black men leaving a bachelor party in Queens, killing 23-year-old Sean Bell on his wedding day. The detectives charged with the crime have since launched a smear campaign against Bell.

In case you're wondering, Ms. Poorman's show is so low-budget she can't afford daycare.

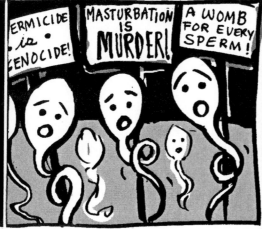

mikhaela reid '06 ★ www.mikhaela.net ★ toons@mikhaela.net

*Excluding homosexual and black sperm.

One of my newspapers spiked this cartoon over the image in the last panel, winning it a home in David Wallis's book *Killed Cartoons: Casualties of the War on Free Expression*. I'm planning to animate this one.

WAR MARKETEERS!

Hello, I'm a U.S. supporter. Occupation forces are Mac-cool!

And I'm an insurgent. Resistance is futile—not to mention dorky!

YOU INGRATES.

We closed our own schools & hospitals to bomb yours!

Sorry!

That we kicked down your door, strip-searched your wife and tortured your kids! Still best friends?

Democracy Rocks!

Dude, at least you got to vote before we accidentally blew up your wedding!

We don't need to try harder to avoid killing, torturing and bombing civilians, we just need to spin it better!

The Afterlife Adventures of Jerry Falwell

Haunting gays, feminists, atheists and ACLU members...

You caused 9/11...

Possessing the body of Mitt Romney

Must... bash... homosexuals...

Kill... Tinky... Winky...

Manifesting as Falwellithor, Eater of Public Schools

That's what you get for teaching evolution, monkey loving secularists!

Hanging with Strom Thurmond in Hell

Civil RIGHTS movement? More like the Civil WRONGS movement!

You tell 'em, sonny!

Falwell is primarily known as a gay-hater and anti-feminist, but he got his start in racism—in 1964, he told a local paper that the Civil Rights Act "should be considered civil wrongs rather than civil rights."

I'm still dreaming. Oh well.

A few months later, the Supreme Court finally ruled in *Lawrence vs. Texas* that sodomy laws were unconstitutional, rendering such pickup lines adorably obsolete.

The military screens all letters, so under "Don't Ask, Don't Tell," gay service members can't communicate openly with their sweethearts for fear of being outed and discharged.

Preparing for the Harsh Realities of War

mikhaela '03 ★ toons@mikhaela.net ★ www.mikhaela.net

Four years later, both the war and *American Idol* are still going like gangbusters.

Most Americans have finally realized what a bloody mistake the Iraq War has been, but instead of a pullout all we've gotten is a surge and some toothless nonbinding resolutions.

Black bars inserted to protect innocent eyes.

...and counting.

mikhaela '03 ★ www.mikhaela.net

Current missing guest list count: 3,278.

When Santorum was under fire for his infamous "man on dog" comments equating homosexuality and bestiality, Bush came to his defense, calling him an "inclusive man."

the Lesson Plan

mikhaela '03
★ www.mikhaela.net ★

WELL CLASS, WE MAY NOT HAVE HAVE ANY MONEY FOR BOOKS OR PAPER THIS YEAR...

AND WE CAN'T PAY ANY OF THE LIBRARIANS OR THE ART TEACHER OR THE COMPUTER TEACHER...

AND YOU CAN FORGET AFTER-SCHOOL CLUBS AND TUTORS.

BUT LUCKY FOR YOU, WE CAN STILL AFFORD TO SPEND...

...A FEW MONTHS TESTING YOU TO SEE HOW MUCH YOU'VE LEARNED.

I've taught a few cartooning workshops for high school students, and I loved every minute of it—certainly much more fun than Cartoon Teacher Mikhaela had in this depressing cartoon!

I later listened to an audio recording of Thurmond's "bayonets" comment and learned he actually used the *other* N-word. After Thurmond's death it was revealed that the die-hard segregationist had fathered a daughter with his 16-year-old black housekeeper in 1925. Trent Lott is now Senate Minority Whip, appropriately enough.

Part of a dystopian "Four More Years" series I did leading up to the 2004 election.

It's not easy being a college gay-hater!

"We have to eat in common halls where our food might be contaminated by faggy cooties!"

"It's hard to study when you're worried your homo roomie might invite you to his gay wedding!"

"Universities DISCRIMINATE against student groups and the military just because we won't let any dirty rugmunchers join!"

"They won't even let us BEAT any fags to work out our anger!"

But fight on, brothers and sisters, and take heart—such dire injustice cannot stand forever!

→ On Thursday, October 3, a beautiful young woman disappeared after attending a party in a San Francisco suburb. Two weeks later her body was found in the Sierra foothills. She had been beaten, strangled, and buried in a

SHALLOW GRAVE

The murdered girl's friends knew her as Gwen Araujo. She was 17 years old.

If this case sounds unfamiliar, you probably saw it reported as...

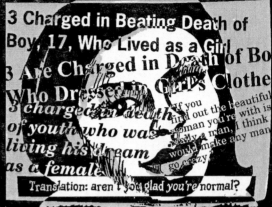

3 Charged in Beating Death of Boy, 17, Who Lived as a Girl

3 Are Charged in Death of Boy Who Dressed in Girl's Clothes

3 charged in death of youth who was living his dream as a female

"If you find out the beautiful woman you're with is really a man, I think it would make any man go crazy."

Translation: aren't you glad you're normal?

Turns out that three boys at the party decided to kill Araujo after they discovered she was biologically male. The other partygoers kept silent for days.

ME! →

I DON'T KNOW IF IT'S MORE IRONIC OR GROSS THAT THE MEDIA INSISTS ON REFERRING TO GWEN AS "HE" + "HIM"

...AT THE SAME TIME AS THEY QUOTE A FRIEND SAYING ARAUJO HATED BEING CALLED "EDDIE" + CONSIDERED HERSELF A GIRL.

Araujo's mother reports that anyone who loved her child called her Gwen — the name she'll put on her daughter's grave.

SO LET THE RECORD STATE: GWEN ARAUJO WAS A TRANSGENDER GIRL MURDERED IN HATRED AND BIGOTRY

IT WON'T BRING HER BACK... BUT AT LEAST IT RESPECTS HER MEMORY.

IN Memory of

...Gwen Araujo ★ Chanelle Pickett ★ Rita Hester ★ Debra Forte ★ Tyra Hunter ★ Cynthia + Felicia Coffman ★ Brandon Teena ★ Marsha P. Johnson ★ Lauryn Paige ★ Fred Martinez, Jr. (aka Fredericka) ★ Nguyen Bui Linh ★ Stephanie Thomas ★ Ukea Davis ★ Della Reeves ★ Billy Jean Lavette ★ Thomas Hall ★ Maria "La Conchita" Palencia ★ Rene "Michelle" Ouellet ★ Tasha Dunn ★ Terrie Ladwig ★ Chrissey (Marvin) Johnson ★ Steven Wilson ★ Christian Paige ★ Vianna Faye Williams ★ Johanna Langer ★ Unknown, Guatemala City, 1997 ★ Robert H. Jones ★ Stacey Estupinian★ Unknown Los Angeles, 1991 ★ Diane Delia ★ Marcela (Sergio Arias) ★ Lisa Janna Black ... and many more.

© mikhaela '02 ★ www.mikhaela.net

*Names courtesy of www.gender.org/remember

This is one of those things you draw while crying. Her attackers used a blame-the-victim "transgender panic" defense, but two were eventually convicted of 2nd-degree murder and the other two of voluntary manslaughter.

The Roving Reporter asks:

If you had $100 billion to make the world a better place, what would you spend it on?

"Cleaning up the air."

"Education."

"Removing land mines."

"Universal health care."

"Fighting AIDS in Africa."

"World peace."

"Bombing the $#*#! out of that guy who tried to hurt my dad."

"Regime change."

Drawn back when there was still hope of preventing the war. At the time $100 billion was considered a "high estimate," but the cost so far has been over $400 billion.

★ www.mikhaela.net

© mikhaela '02

Super-Duper Quick & Easy Guide to

How Much You Love Hitler!

You know you worship totalitarianism if...

The surveillance camera in your colon gives you a tummy-ache.

You know you yearn for the good old days of slavery if...

You're horrified by secret CIA torture prisons.

You know you're a Nazi-kissing swastika collector if...

BRING MY BROTHER HOME NOW

You don't want any more troops to die over non-existent WMDs.

You know you're Osama's boot-licking love bunny if...

You mourn the deaths of tens of thousands of innocent civilians.

You know you're a fascist when... you protest fascism.

trend TRACKER
CONSERVATIVE SPRING STYLES

RUNWAY Rx.

BLACK GOLD IS THE NEW BLACK.
Show off your crude attitude with a daily regimen of perfectly pretty petroleum. Non-fossil fuels need not apply! Guzzlicious!

$75 a barrel—and rising!

VIAGRA (sildenafil citrate) tablets

Republican rappers rep Big Pharma! Pfizer in the House—of Style!*

Schoolhouse Frocks.
Mandatory abstinence-promotion uniforms for female pupils of all ages! Purity with panache!

Penis-vagina contact before marriage causes suicide!

Stars and... Style!
Rotating flag with built-in level for proper patriotism! Take that, illegals!

"What global warming?" Block out harmful reality rays!

mikhaela reid '06 • www.mikhaela.net • toons@mikhaela.net   *I actually saw a guy wearing this last week.

After seeing a man in a Viagra-branded NASCAR jacket, I toyed with the idea of embarrassing pharmaceutical fashions (such as pants with "Ex-Lax" written in rhinestones on the rear) but wound up with this.

Talking *Doll*

A recent poll on Barbie.com allowed children three gender choices—boy, girl, and "I don't know"—proof, according to a spokesman for the Concerned Women for America, of Mattel's dangerous "bisexuality gender confusion" agenda.

OK, OK, I admit it. Since time immemorial, I have been a willing pawn of the global transgender conspiracy...

Ceaseless in my sick quest to force young children to stray from their safe and natural gender roles through contact with tacky fluorescent dressup ensembles...

All with the eventual aim of raising a army of polyamorous feminist transsexual bisexual gender confusion terrorists with a mutual love of pink princesses and missing plastic genitalia...

But I'm a reformed girl now and shall henceforth be content...

To be a normal, healthy, plastic doll with a tiny waist and huge boobs in a fairy bride costume.

Let's go to the mall!

Mattel quickly removed the "I don't know" option, but I still find it hilarious that the *man* representing Concerned *Women* for America was so worried about "gender confusion."

Sick of your kids being exposed to storybook "tolerance" propaganda like the gay-themed *King & King*? Why not demand that schools teach *Help! Mom! There Are Liberals Under My Bed!* and other fine

Conservative Children's Classics

Help! Dad! Mommy is a Deluded Feminist Who Thinks She Can Have a Career AND a Family!
by Caitlin Flanagan

King & King Go to Ex-Gay Therapy to Shake Off the Shackles of the Global Homosexual Agenda
by Dr. J. Dobson

The Lorax Realizes that Global Warming is a Lie Propagated by Ecoterrorists
by Michael Crichton

The Little Smart Bomb That Could
by Don Rumsfeld

Working mother Caitlin Flanagan made time for a writing career denouncing working mothers—and lauding traditional marriage, housework and child-rearing—by hiring housecleaning staff and a full-time nanny.

As the punk band Dead Kennedys once put it: "Give me convenience or give me death!"

The Super-Duper Quick + Easy Guide to
Becoming a Hard-Hitting Journalist
Too busy for J-school? This is all you need to know.

#1 Present both sides of an issue fairly.

Some scientists say the earth is round. But a guy I know says they're just a bunch of crackpot liberal elitists. Who's right? It's impossible to say.

THE FLAT EARTH DEBATE

#2 Ask tough questions.

Mr. President, isn't it true that you are a pure force for good and Democrats are evil aliens from the Planet Zorkathon?

#3 Cultivate good relationships with key sources.

We'll pay you $240,000 to promote No Child Left Behind.

Sure, why not?

#4 Aw, heck, who am I kidding? Just get yourself a web site.

Puny "old media" journalists will bow down before my amazing powers of snarky criticism.

The Liberty Spreader.com

Dude, Ann Coulte is soo much hote then those Dem crat chicks.

Conservatives look at the brighter side of... Hurricane Katrina

The evangelical Christian group Repent America claimed that God destroyed New Orleans to stop the Southern Decadence gay pride festival. Also, Bush ate cake with John McCain while New Orleans drowned.

Bush + Cheney's Super-Duper Quick + Easy Guide to
Conservation!

FEATURING LIGHTBULB HEAD ED!

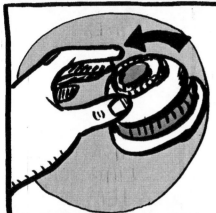

TURN DOWN that thermostat on your way to drilling in the Arctic National Wildlife Refuge!

BUY AN ENERGYSTAR FRIDGE before you gut fuel-efficiency standards!

MAKE SURE YOU install insulated windows when ignoring the overwhelming scientific evidence of global warming!

DON'T FORGET to replace those energy-hogging incandescent bulbs before you start your next illegal oil war!

Conservation, Bush-style: politely encourage individuals to voluntarily turn down their thermostats a smidge while letting big corporations pollute all they want.

Remember Tom Ridge and his color-coded terror alerts?

Medical Malpractice

by a quaint mikhaela '04 ★ www.mikhaela.net ★ toons@mikhaela.net

Out of the John Ashcroft frying pan, into the Alberto Gonzales fire:
Bush's second Attorney General called the Geneva Conventions "quaint."

OWNERSHIP ★ SOCIETY!!!

We plan to take great pride in owning even larger insurance premiums and hospital bills.

I'll finally be able to own a more extensive collection of unpaid credit card statements.

I can't wait to own another pair of scissors to clip out coupons with.

We'll happily continue to own a million times as much as the rest of the people in this cartoon put together.

I haven't heard this slogan in a while—it must have tested poorly.

Back in June 2004, Bush was making a big fuss about how independent and sovereign Iraq was.

Well, Wasn't That Fun?

So it's 5 a.m. Wednesday morning and I can't say for sure who won.

What I can say is that millions of Americans braved bad weather and long lines...

... nobly determined to exercise their sacred democratic right...

... to stop gay people from marrying and give the popular vote to a lying, trigger-happy madman.

Some post-2004 election good cheer, self-portrait style. I don't know why I bother to stay up anymore.

Election time in Afghanistan.

FOUR MORE YEARS: THE ENVIRONMENT

Some tips from President Bush on turning our stressful, cluttered environment into a peaceful, zenlike refuge.

1. Make Room for a View
Removing unsightly forests and mountaintops provides an optimal view of smog-enhanced sunsets.

2. Clear Critter Clutter
How many owl species does one planet really need?

3. Add Architecture
Oil rigs bring a lovely baroque touch to any Arctic skyline and make use of space normally wasted on caribou.

4. Cut Noise Pollution
Silencing scientists who talk about global warming creates calm and quiet.

5. Relax and Enjoy!
Congratulations—you've converted billions of years of clutter into a modern, minimalist masterpiece.

Bush gets all Martha Stewart on the planet.

FEAR · FACTORS

When I heard about mad cow, I stopped eating beef. When I read the statistics on divorce, I stopped dating.

I stay away from Florida because of the hurricanes, California because of the quakes and Texas because of the tornadoes.

Since 9/11, I've avoided airplanes and tall buildings.

Now I can't decide which is more dangerous: driving, or taking the subway?

So I bought some bottled water and duct tape and locked myself in.

Whatever happens, I'm ready.

After the July 2005 London bombings. This isn't me, but as a nine-year-old I did develop a deep (if not particularly long-lived) fear of the entire state of California after seeing the '89 San Francisco quake on TV.

It's hard out there for a racist stereotype! These costumes would fit in just fine at those awful blackface parties that are all the rage at retrograde college frats lately.

Not making this up: exit polls indicate 23% of self-identified gay voters went for Bush in both 2000 and 2004. Clearly due to the magnetic charms of James Dobson and Jerry Falwell.

INSIDE THE SICK WORLD OF A SERIAL BOMBER

Somewhere in a parallel universe...

Tonight on ZNN: a chilling account of lies, torture, and groundless war.

Parents should be advised that the following footage is extremely graphic.

ZNN

"Neighbors remember the former Cub scout as a family man, father of two, and frequent churchgoer."

How could we have known he'd sacrifice 100,000 Iraqis and 1,700 Americans in a sick hunt for imaginary WMDs?

ZNN

"But serial bomber experts say he displayed all the classic signs."

It was all right there: disdain for democracy, detachment from reality, an insatiable lust for power and oil.

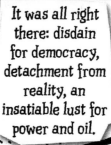 

ZNN

"Survivors say they are glad he is being brought to justice, but even justice cannot repair their shattered lives."

I relive it every moment—the noise, the flash, my daughter and husband crushed under the falling ceiling...

ZNN

"At his trial, Bush showed no remorse or empathy for his victims, referring to the mass killings with clinical terms such as 'preemptive strike' and 'liberation.'"

ZNN

The monster's reign of lies and death is at an end, but across America tonight, the question lingers: why didn't we see the signs sooner?

ZNN

What if serial bombers got the same media treatment as serial killers?

the ABC's of AIDS

A Primer for Proper Ladies and Gentlemen Around the World

you must **A**bstain from sex...

So I can Be faithful to my right-wing religious base...

who aren't very fond of **C**ondoms and sex education

And if that doesn't work, you can always just **D**ie.

mikhaela '04 ★ www.mikhaela.net

88

DEMOCRATIC·UNITY

My embarrassingly sentimental reaction to the first official same-sex weddings in Massachusetts. That's Bush and Romney crying in anger in the middle bottom panel.

Donald "I'm not going to address the torture word" Rumsfeld presents:

PENTAGON
memo comics

When Saddam did it...

Torture

When we do it...

Intelligence-gathering techniques vital to the preservation of national security

Even after the Abu Ghraib scandal broke and a Rumsfeld-penned memo advocating torture surfaced, Bush still claimed that one of the justifications for the Iraq war was that Saddam tortured people.

There's so much to say, and so little space in which to say it...

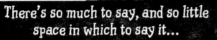

baby me!

I loved her right from the start.

When I was little, she took me for walks in the Maine woods...

Why can't we play with the nice doggy* Grandmommy?

* Big black bear.

My brother and I used to just sit and read with her for hours and hours and hours...

Max me

She read (at least) a book a day.

When I got older, she taught me all about knitting and sewing...

Ta-da!

Oh, nice honey, very nice!

floor-length gown!

And did I mention she loved bright colors, country music, *Law & Order*, and hummingbirds? That she served in the Air Force during the Korean War? That she was really looking forward to voting against Bush in November? That she was from Pickwick, Tennessee? That when Max was little he used to sneak into her room late at night, curl up in her lap and eat candy without my parents' permission?

in loving memory

Melba Ruby Reid (Shipman)

born Jan. 31, 1931 died March 23, 2004

mikhaela '04 ★ www.mikhaela.net

I drew this cartoon the night my grandmother died. She was a huge fan of political cartoonists, especially Bill Mauldin, Garry Trudeau, Dan Wasserman and me. I wish she could have seen herself in the newspaper.

All across America, people are touched by

Bush's Support for the Troops

mikhaela '03 ★ www.mikhaela.net

Past...

"I'm touched by the letter I got asking me to give back part of my benefits check."

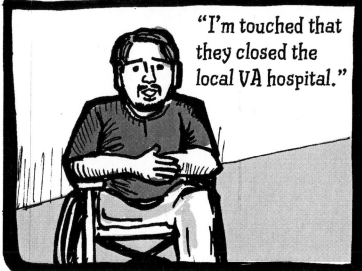

"I'm touched that they closed the local VA hospital."

"I'm touched that my husband didn't have a bullet-proof vest when he was attacked."

...and Present

My grandmother Melba was a retired disabled veteran (see facing page) who relied on her small monthly VA check. Not long before she died, she received a letter asking her to give back part of her benefits.

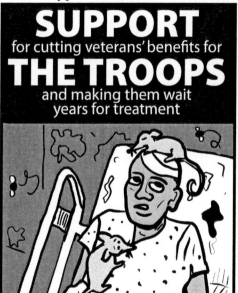

In case it's not clear, he's holding a credit card, not a condom.

I had way too many My Little Pony dolls as a child.

Bill! Has it been 15 years already? Damn fine job, as always! You're the best engineer we've got!

Give positive feedback!

Hell, without your dedication and innovative spirit, I don't know how we'd manage! I'll make sure you get the big raise and promotion you deserve!

Now what was it you had to tell me?

Reward top performers.

Ed, I'm transsexual. In the next few months I'll be transitioning to live as a woman and changing my name to Beth. Is there an HR process I need to—

Security!

Be a good listener.

But you said—

Sorry, "Bill" — your "Old Boys Club" membership just expired!

Always work within the law!

Longtime Largo, Fla., City Manager Steve Stanton was fired after announcing plans to transition to life as Susan Stanton. In much of the U.S. employers have free reign to discriminate against gay, lesbian, bisexual and transgender people. The moral? We need a national employment non-discrimination act, like, yesterday.

Current reputable estimates of Iraqi civilian casualties range from 61,000-650,000.

If You're Not With Us...
⇒ A BUSH + BUDDIES QUIZ

Q Which of the following are NOT terrorist groups?

1

2

3

REAL SEX ED SAVES LIVES

PRO-CHOICE PRO-CHILD

KEEP ABORTION LEGAL

Brown v. Board · equal

PRO-CHOICERS
Protested restrictions on access to family planning and abortion

TEACHERS
Criticized under-funded No Child Left Behind Act

HIJACKERS
Flew planes into buildings, killing thousands

ER... COULD SOMEONE GIVE ME A HINT?

Sure! Bush adviser Karen Hughes recently compared pro-choicers to the "terror network we fight." And Education Secretary Rod Paige has called the largest teachers' union a "terrorist organization." No joke.

Teachers are the *REAL* terrorists!

asking · for · it

THEN...

Those boys had no choice but to beat, torture, and hang that Negro for winking at one of our women—any NORMAL man would have done the same.

Of course I'm against lynching —but why should my children be forced to go to school with THOSE people?

NOW...

Those boys had no choice but to beat, torture, and strangle that girl after they discovered she was a tranny—any NORMAL man would have done the same.

Of course that murder was horrible—but that doesn't mean I want my children to learn about that SICK LIFESTYLE in school.

The last panel is inspired by cases in which transgender parents have faced harassment and abuse from other parents for offering to volunteer their time as chaperones and volleyball coaches.

Bush initially offered only $15 million to help victims of the deadly 2004 tsunami—
not much more than the $11 million we spend on screwing up Iraq every hour.

RETURN OF THE ROVING REPORTER!

What do you think about the forced registration of men from Middle Eastern countries?

mikhaela '03 ★ www.mikhaela.net

"Big Brother is watching you."

"Same way they treated my parents during World War II."

"Don't even get me started."

"It's a load of fascist bull$*!#."

"I'm not exactly shocked."

"Gosh, I feel soooo much safer now!"

"I haven't seen my youngest son in three days."

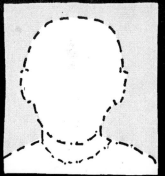

Not available for comment.

After 9/11, the feds detained thousands of men whose only crime was being Arab, Muslim or South Asian. Many were confined without charges for weeks or months, and/or deported.

When Romney tried to win Ted Kennedy's Senate seat in 1994, he claimed he was pro-gay and pro-choice. Kennedy shot back that Romney was really "Multiple Choice."

While I'm on a Mitt-bashing kick: The ACLU of Massachusetts bought the original of this one.

Black History Month • Moment #371

Earl shares a story from back in the day when crooked Southern politicians denied blacks their right to vote

mikhaela '03 ★ www.mikhaela.net

"...And that's why Grandma and I don't live in Florida anymore."

I'm referring to the stolen 2000 election, of course, when many black voters in Florida were turned away from polling places—or purged from the rolls for having the same last names as convicted felons.

"W stands for women" was an actual Bush 2004 campaign slogan.

GOOD NEWS!

This just in! Our wise and brave President Bush says that man/woman marriage will spread democracy in the Middle East and fix Social Security.

Unfortunately, our courageous leader faces opposition from selfish hedonist homosexuals. For more on this alarming story, we turn to Bob Jones.

Thanks Lisa! White House officials confirm that bisexual terrorist AARP members have joined with the ACLU and NAACP to destroy America.

Better hide your kids, folks—they recruit! Be sure to join us tomorrow when we turn our unbiased eye on the Nazis who want to prevent drilling in the Arctic!

mikhaela '05 ★ www.mikhaela.net ★ toons@mikhaela.net

My take on the White-House-produced "video news releases" getting passed off as journalism on local stations.

Not-So-Great Moments in Black History

 # 829: Bush tries to sell African Americans on his Social Security plan by claiming it will benefit black men who die young

In yet another clumsy attempt to woo black voters, Bush claimed his plan to privatize Social Security would benefit black men because they tend to die too young to get the most out of existing Social Security coverage.

After the 2004 coup in Haiti, Bush immediately deployed the Coast Guard—to keep refugees from the violence from escaping, that is.

Their intervention in the Schiavo case is just one reason why people across the nation are deeply moved by Bush & friends' *Respect for Life*

I'm moved by the way they cut health care for poor children in their budget...

And the cutting food stamps thing, that was sweet too.

Nothing warms my heart like the way they outsource the torture of prisoners to Syria, Jordan, Morocco and Egypt.

Except for when they torture people themselves.

I don't know what comforts my soul more— lethal injection, electrocution, or the gas chamber?

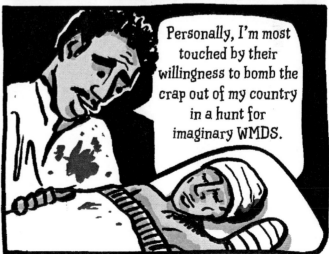

Personally, I'm most touched by their willingness to bomb the crap out of my country in a hunt for imaginary WMDS.

Some of you may be laboring under the impression that the Bush administration lied about weapons of mass destruction to win support for a war that has killed thousands of Iraqis and Americans. You poor, misled fools!

NEWSWEEK: The Real Killers!

Did you think those missiles that fell on Baghdad were fired by the U.S. military? I bet you didn't know they were actually set off by NEWSWEEK!

Did you think Bush would knowingly put American kids in harm's way? Well, he didn't really know— NEWSWEEK fed him crazy pills!

Did you know that Lynndie England is actually an android built by NEWSWEEK? That pregnancy thing was a nice touch!

NEWSWEEK even hung a Mission Accomplished banner behind the president —before the mission was accomplished!

The Bush administration blamed a poorly sourced *Newsweek* story about guards at Gitmo abusing the Koran for violence and anti-U.S. sentiment in the Muslim world.

Many staunchly Reagan-loathing liberal cartoonists grew mysteriously fond of him when he died and depicted him eating jellybeans in Heaven. They should have drawn him eating ketchup.

Remember when Iraq was a "victory in the War on Terror"?

News Item: 12 discharged gay veterans sue for reinstatement in the military

Patriotism, Pentagon-Style

Those guys crack me up.

How would you feel if no one remembered your name?

Hey, Andrea, how's it going?

If bathrooms were danger zones?

GET BEAT UP

GET SCREAMED AT

If apartments, jobs and respect were always mysteriously unavailable?

Job posting? Are you joking?

HELP WANTED.

If your "friends" strangled and beat you to death when they learned you were transgender, and their lawyers blamed YOU?

Gwen Araujo
★ 1985-2002 ★

· Make · it · Stop ·

 mikhaela '04 ★ www.mikhaela.net

118

STRANGE, BUT TRUE...

Despite departure of Jayson Blair, American papers still found to contain lies, exaggerations and unverified facts...

The Daily Times

Tax Cuts for Wealthy Will Help Needy, Create Jobs, Walk on Water, Says Bush

"Can I have more money for bombs, please?"

TOP GUN: PRESIDENT BUSH

Rebuilding Iraq Going Just Fine, Says White House

"Weapons of Mass Destruction? I'm afraid we have no idea what the hell you're referring to."

Civil Liberties Not Being Curtailed by John Ashcroft, Says Attorney General

"Anyone who thinks otherwise is an enemy combatant."

mikhaela '03 ★ www.mikhaela.net

Opponents of the cervical cancer vaccine speak out!

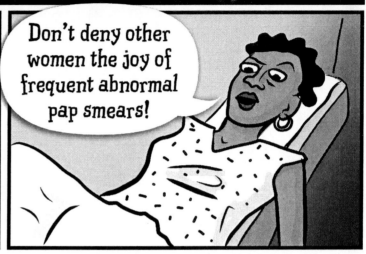

When I drew this, the loudest anti-vaccine voices were moral values types. Since then, questions have been raised about Merck's over-zealous marketing campaign, and the HPV vaccine's efficacy against cervical cancer.

A Bush tribute to Martin Luther King, Jr.

I have a dream that all the oil of Iraq will rise up and pour into our reserves, and that every Iraqi will show proper gratitude to his liberators.

I have a dream that in the grand mansions and big corporations of this land, no one shall pay any taxes.

I have a dream that one day the killers of innocent stem cells will be fried in the electric chair.

I have a dream that one day my two children will live in a nation where man-woman marriage is mandatory and all homosexuals are sent to Guantánamo Bay.

And I have a really big dream that one day black folks will forget that Hurricane Katrina business and vote Republican.

Let freedom to torture ring!

FUNDAMENTALIST BOOT CAMP

WITH SGT. DOBSON!

ROMNEY! GIULIANI! WHAT'S THIS I HEAR ABOUT YOU BEING GAY-LOVING BABY-KILLING STEM-CELL SQUASHERS?

DROP AND GIVE ME 50!

Abortion is murder! Abortion is murder! Abortion is...

Er... 9/11?

Homosexuals are a threat to the American family!

SHAPE UP, ADULTEREROUS SCUM—OR I MIGHT JUST TELL EVANGELICALS TO VOTE FOR THAT GOSH-DARNED MORMON!

Sir, YES SIR!

Traditional marriage...

...is between...

...one man...

...and one woman!

Giuliani hasn't done a Romney cartwheel on abortion yet, but he has started talking about "marriage between a man and a woman." He also recently expressed support for a "state's right" to fly the Confederate Flag.

After years of Mitt Romney (and Jane Swift and Paul Cellucci and William Weld), Democrat Deval Patrick's win in Massachusetts was like waking up from a long, strange, nasty dream.

What are YOU proud of?

At long last, bigots share their shining moments of gloriousness!

"I own 5,431 anti-immigrant beer coasters. Take that, illegals!"

I'm stitching up an "AIDS is how God annihilates the fags and the blacks" quilt!

WE'RE HERE, WE HATE QUEERS* GET USED TO IT!
*& BABYKILLING FEMINAZIS, MEXICANS, ~IN-LOVERS, ARABS, GODLESS ~LS, ENVIROTERRORISTS, REALITY

We stopped speaking to our darling son when he brought home an ETHNIC lady.

I lobbied day and night, snow and sun, rain and shine to get a transsexual parent kicked out of the PTA!

I crash homo weddings with my six-piece Ex-Gay Marching Band of Truth!

Behind every Bush administration public image disaster lurks...

MILLY JONES

AMERICA-HATING PR REPRESENTATIVE

Guantánamo suicides

OK people—let's see a little more gut-wrenching despair here!

Civilian casualties in Iraq

Remember: run TOWARDS the falling bombs! The more limbs you lose, the better the anti-American PR!

Abu Ghraib

Baby, you're a STAR!

Hurricane Katrina

Make sure you don't get rescued for at least four days—it'll make a great PR stunt!

Why, if it weren't for that scheming scandal-monger, we'd all know Bush for the competent and caring man he truly is!

A top Bush spokes-idiot called three suicides at Gitmo "a good PR move to draw attention."
A little research turned up the genius behind this bit of Extreme Public Relations.

Bush no longer asks for *war* funding, he asks for "funding to protect our troops in harm's way."
Otherwise known as "funding to get our troops killed for no damn reason."

HOT STORIES OF 2007!!!

RELIGION!!!

Jerry Falwell, James Dobson and Fred Phelps caught running gay prostitution/drug ring; followers heartbroken.

"The homosexual agenda *sniff* strikes again!"

SCANDAL!!!

Lou Dobbs' plan to build border wall from apple pie and American flags loses support when he is revealed to be a Martian overlord in a cheap mask.

BRAVERY!!!

If elected, Hillary vows to pull out of Iraq so she can invade, bomb and occupy the country "the right way."

COMEBACKS!!!

Bush regains popularity with documentary "The Truth About How the Clean Air Fairies Turn Pollution Into Daisies and Lemon Drops."

I firmly believe that Lou Dobbs is an evil Martian overlord. You'll see!

It's hard out there for a self-centered traitor.

★ *Brighter Side of Middle East Violence!* ★

Oh, I think we're having some VERY productive conversations!

Some civilians may be getting mixed up in the fighting, but we must have a SUSTAINABLE ceasefire!

These truly lovely progressive conversations are sure to lead to lots of darling progress!

Let's have another productive conversation again soon!

Ms. Rice had a (glass) "half-full" mentality about the bombing of Lebanon.

Mr. Bush's Cryogenically Frozen Friendship Hour!

The president's precious pearls of embryonic wisdom!

Before you raise the fruits of another woman's womb, consider adopting an adorable frozen embryo of your very own!

The lives of discarded embryos are valuable and precious—unlike the lives of Iraqis and death-row inmates!

The mean Parkinson's patients tried to sell Sammy Stem Cell to Science...

But the brave president stopped them with his magic veto!

MY PET STEM CELL

The only bad frozen embryo... is a same-sex married frozen embryo!

Like Mr. Rogers, only in a laboratory telling stories to stem cells.

Someone get that guy a Pulitzer.

HOLIDAY GIFTS
for defeated Republicans

Turn election frowns upside down!

HOT GAME!

Super-realistic "Cakewalk 2003" for Wintendo Frii. Catch flowers from grateful Iraqis!

HOT BOOK!

LIBERALS: *Traitorous Terrorists or Terrorist Traitors?*

HOT TOY! Torture Me Elmo

♪ ♫ **HOT CD!**

Features classics like "Tis the Season to Blow up Godless Secular Humanist Malls" and "Deck the Halls with the Crushed Entrails of Bill O'Reilly's Enemies!"

War on Christmas Carols

HOT LUXURY!

wink

Discreet massage and pharmaceutical service for that special closeted anti-gay leader in your life. *Ask for the Ted Haggard special!*

Next week: Gifts for Victorious Democrats!
Backbones and more!

This whole cartoon was just an excuse for a random *Project Runway* joke. Warmongering is so tacky!

Number two in a very occasional series.

Pushy homos and uppity females getting you down? Why not cloak your hate in faith and say:

It's My Religion!

BEFORE...

Gosh, I sure wish I could scare those dirty little dykes, but I don't want to get in trouble...

DAY OF SILENCE

HATE ISN'T A FAMILY VALUE

AFTER!

Hey! It's my religion!

HOMOSEXUALS ARE SHAMEFUL

MATTHEW SHEPHARD IS FICTIONAL

My faith doesn't allow me to fill prescriptions for HARLOTS!

Stop infringing my rights, you orgy-crazed trollop!

Hold on, folks... I'm receiving a transmission from the Lord...

He says to bomb the Iraqis, nuke Iran and stop man-man weddin's!

WARNING: If your faith leads you to advocate love, peace, civil rights, gay rights, women's rights and/or social justice, please stop praying immediately and consult your local Focus on the Family.

A conservative student backed by the Family Research Council sued his public school for the right to wear a "Homosexuality is Shameful" shirt. The FRC claimed the school was violating the boy's religious freedom— and that the antigay murder of Matthew Shephard was "fictional."

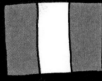

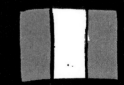

Concerned citizens against earned citizenship laws speak out

My granddaddy didn't make the long and perilous boat trip to these shining shores so that his descendents would be surrounded by funny-talking taco eaters!

AMERICA NOT AMERIC

But if I had to pay my gardeners real wages, what would become of my sweet, innocent prize-winning orchids? Who speaks for THEM?

What's wrong with our current system? These people do jobs Americans aren't willing to do...

Not for what I'm willing to pay them, anyway.

I just know the nanny is plotting Mexican world domination.

Bonus Quiz!

Which of these flags is NOT an acceptable expression of cultural pride?

A. Italian

B. Mexican

C. Irish

The Little Black Book for Young Homosexuals

v. 3.0

★ *Obscene Literature* ★

Conservative Christians are concerned that gay youth could be harmed by exposure to explicit sex ed materials. Thankfully, they have a healthier alternative:

DID YOU KNOW: using condoms during sodomy will actually speed your trip to Hell?

Do you feel lonely and think about hurting yourself sometimes? That's normal and healthy—the world is better off without you, you nasty little dyke!

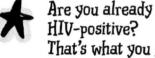

Are you already HIV-positive? That's what you get for being a faggot!

Biblical scholars have discovered that Jesus *REALLY* said "Love thy neighbor— *UNLESS* he is homosexual or transsexual!"

Sex is only for married straight people who find each other very yucky naked but want to make babies for God!

Want to escape burning in the fiery pits with me for all eternity? Ask your parents to send you to a reparative therapist!

Being ex-gay is A-OK!

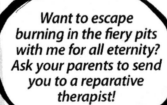

Give me your tired, your poor... (sort of)

A MOTHER'S STORY*

→ In 1977, the Khmer Rouge took her oldest son to the killing fields.

←In 1976, water poisoned by corpses made her youngest daughter ill.

↑ In 1975, the Khmer Rouge took Sophea's husband for "reeducation."

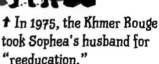

→ In 1978, her middle son collapsed from starvation in a work camp.

↑ In 1979, her last daughter succumbed to malnutrition just before reaching the refugee camp in Thailand.

→ In 2002, the US government bullied Cambodia into accepting 1,400 deportees convicted of "aggravated felonies" (including shoplifting, marijuana possession, and drunk driving)**. Many of these refugees had already served their time, had US-born children, and/or were the primary providers for their families. Among them was her youngest son.

*Although this story is a composite, it is unfortunately not atypical. An estimated 2 million Cambodians (1/4 of the population) perished under Pol Pot's brutal regime. Some 145,000 survivors came to the US as refugees.

**Basically, this is a result of post 9/11 anti-immigrant sentiment + the 1996 Immigration Act. Under the Act, judges have no discretion to halt deportations even under extenuating circumstances—such as the fact that many of the deportees can't read or write Khmer, or that many of their "felonies" were relatively minor crimes, typically punished by sentences of five years or less.

My first all-digital cartoon, and the first one I did using the font I designed to replace my sloppy hand-lettering. I was thrilled when an anti-deportation group asked to use it in posters and buttons for a rally.

"Global warming? In my day, we called this a refreshing spring breeze!"

My counter to conservative cartoons featuring wise grandparents telling the kiddies that "global warming" is just a new-fangled phrase for "summer."

Fun + Funky Freedom Facts!

Freedom is a marvelous colorless gas smelling slightly of licorice, best distilled from:

Bald eagle droppings

The screams of tortured detainees

Although freedom can be spread on toast, for most potent effect it must be taken in bomb form.

People all over the world love the clean refreshing taste of freedom.

FREEDOM is totally LOVELY!

Freedom lovers know only freedom haters actually USE freedom.

My fellow Americans, we are

Too Darn Healthy!

For too long, we have taken advantage of easily available care!

Dude, let's get go get expensive unnecessary colonoscopies!

Without the crutch of insurance, we'd make wiser chocies!

Baby, I really think I should see a doctor...

Too bad you blew our money on RENT and UTILITIES.

We have been denied the freedom of comparison shopping!

Boutique Rx

Spa + Luxe massage

WAL★DOC!

LOW PRICE!

Now just an 8 hour wait!

GUY WITH A SAW!

2 LEGS 4 PRICE OF 1!!

Health Savings Accounts: Because America needs more untreated cancer!

he! he!

Who needs health insurance when Guy With a Saw's prices are so darn reasonable?

YOUR YUCKY BODY
summer swimsuit spectacular!

DEEPEST CLEANSING PORE STRIPPERS

BEFORE   AFTER

Summer and sand can scrape the skin, so put a stop to sun damage with sweet-scented nose removal strips!

BEAUTY BUZZ MOISTURE RAZOR Gently removes excess hair, dead skin, genitalia.

ULTRA TAN GOO
Get a healthy deep pumpkin flush or die of pasty pasty shame.*

*Fab Fairness Goo available for overly dusky "ethnic" ladies!

GOLD CHASTITY BIKINI

ORAL CELLULITE SERUM
Do the honorable thing and put an end to jiggly thighs—for eternity.

GOP leaders did a heckuva job covering up Mark Foley's dirty emails to underage pages. But there's plenty of perfidy they haven't pushed under the rug!

More NASTY Republican Messages.

Scared_Detainee81

General_AlGonzo55: can't wait until you are all tied up and beaten like a slave

Scared_Detainee81: please stop let me go home i am innocent how can this be legal

General_AlGonzo55: cuz Congress says so

BrokeSngleMama368

KingGeorgie101: so did U mesur it 4 me yet?

BrokeSngleMama368: measure what?

KingGeorgie101: that big juicy tax cut I gave U

BrokeSngleMama368: you must be confusing me with IncrediblyRichDude368

Stuck_in_Iraq2730

RumStud1984: hey soldier, what r u wearing?

Stuck_in_Iraq2730: a bodybag, you @$&*(+@!!!!

I registered for all these AOL screen names or made them too long to be real. I tried quite a few variations on "Stuck_In_Iraq" before hitting on one that was still available—the number of soldiers killed to date.

Drawing this cartoon was satisfying, but bittersweet—Rumsfeld and Santorum were cartoon gold mines.

Part 2
ODDS & ENDS
COMMISSIONS, ILLUSTRATIONS, STUFF

WARTIME ABC's

by Mikhaela B. Reid

mikhaela '03 ★ toons@mikhaela.net ★ www.mikhaela.net

A is for Ashcroft, and his red pen,

B is for Bunker, Dick's hiding again!

C is for Contract, the rebuilding kind,

D is for Democrats, missing a spine.

E's for the Election that got us to this place,

F is for Fire, with a Friendly Face.

G is for God, on everyone's side,

H is for Homeland, grab duct tape and hide!

I's for Iraqis, living in fear,

J is for Journalism, balanced and fair.

K's for kids not coming home, and their kids,

L's for Liberation—of oil, that is.

With apologies to Edward Gorey. I did this as a commission for *The Boston Phoenix* in 2003, and most of it still holds true four years later except the "Saddam nowhere in sight" bit. Ted Rall has the original in his office.

ITTY-BITTY PAYCHECK

Help college grads Tim and Tara navigate their way to sensational salaries!

A recent piece for
Bitch: Feminist Response to Pop Culture magazine

FUN PAGES!

by Mikhaela Reid
with help from E.J. Graff

Science Bob Says:

"Your crazy ovaries explain why women's wages have been stuck at 77 cents to the average man's dollar for the last decade!"

Silly Uterus Comix:

"So when's the bun going to pop out of your oven and put you on my not-eligible-for-promotion list?"

For more facts, see **Getting Even: Why Women Still Don't Get Paid Like Men—and What To Do About It**, by Evelyn Murphy with E.J. Graff.

Mikhaela Reid is a Brooklyn-based freelance political cartoonist.

E.J. Graff is a senior researcher at the Brandeis Institute for Investigative Journalism.

UNCONSCIOUS DISCRIMINATION FUNNIES

I'm afraid Bill's not in yet.

Probably stuck in traffic, poor guy! Have Ana do it.

She's late, too.

Why doesn't she just stay home with her f$&*# kids?!

Find the right slot for Peggy!

Peggy's a tough gal with three kids and an unemployed husband to feed. Which career should she choose to least offend male coworkers with her wacky female hormones?

ELECTRICIAN	FIRE FIGHTER	WAITRESS
$37,000 a year	$45,000 a year	$18,000 a year

"TOO MUCH, TOO FAST, TOO SOON!"

A primer for pushy homosexual, bisexual and transgendered folk

Watch Your Mouth
Loose lips lose elections!

TOO MUCH
"Hey hey, ho ho, this homophobia has got to go!"

MUCH BETTER
"Er, um, excuse us but do you think perhaps you could possibly accord us some small protections at some point (if it's not too inconvenient for you and doesn't offend moral values voters, of course)."

✓ ✗ Do's and Don'ts

DO vote for us.

DON'T expect us to have the spine to actually stand up and support you and your families. After all, that might not be politically expedient!

A Quick Quiz for Queers

When is it appropriate to agitate for LGBT rights?

a) not now—there's an election coming up
b) not now—can't you see Americans just aren't ready?
c) maybe soon, we'll see
d) no, not yet—there's another election coming up

Remember!
Gay rights victories make a great scapegoat!

Commission for the San Francisco Pride parade magazine, *Inside Pride*. California Senator Diane Feinstein received the parade's 2005 "Pink Brick" award for blaming Bush's "re-election" on the push for marriage equality. She told reporters it "has been too much, too fast, too soon."

I designed the typeface I use in most of my cartoons in a super-fun digital type design class I took at the Rhode Island School of Design with genius Font Bureau designer Cyrus Highsmith. Hand lettering was never my strong suit.

A 2004 cover illustration for *In These Times*. The puppets are the president, prime minister and vice presidents of the newly "sovereign" Iraqi interim government. Above is one of the rejected sketches and a photo of the little paper stage I built as a lighting reference.

2004 Bush Supreme
Court "fold-in" cover for
Bay Windows. Folded, it's
a court bench, unfolded
it's a bed.

Recent cover of *Metro Times*, for a story called "Bringing Down Rumsfeld."

My sketchbook provides a welcome respite from drawing Bush and Cheney's ugly mugs. Technically this is my knitting/crafting group, but we're really more of a political think tank.

Lambda Legal's LIFE WITHOUT FAIR COURTS

Protect Your Rights — Stand Up For Fair Courts! • www.lambdalegal.org/courtingjustice

From an 11-part "Life Without Fair Courts" cartoon series I drew for Lambda Legal, imagining what life would be like today if courts had not upheld the Constitution in landmark cases. This is the "What would life be like without *Brown vs. Board of Education*?" cartoon.

Lambda Legal (lambdalegal.org) does litigation and education work aimed at achieving civil rights for LGBT people and people with HIV. Their success in *Lawrence vs. Texas* brought an end to anti-gay "sodomy laws" in 2003.

Drawn for *Women's eNews* (womensenews.org). Note the reference to the red-sash-wearing Junior Anti-Sex League from George Orwell's *1984*. I dressed up as a League member for Halloween once, complete with fake Newspeak dictionary and navy blue coverall with "Ministry of Truth" stenciled on the back.

PART 3
THE EARLY YEARS

Good-bye giaraffe.
Good-bye Mikhayla.

He eats all the giraffes because he is a giraffe.

Long before clip-art web comics captured the hearts of Americans everywhere, I was a pioneer of the "googly-eyed sticker comics" form. This piece, penned at the tender age of 2 1/2, is a cynical commentary on life in a giraffe-eat-giraffe capitalist consumer culture. (Transcription services kindly provided by my father).

My first published editorial cartoon, from the December 1996 edition of the Lowell High School *Review*. As a punk rock girl, I objected to a stricter new dress code, and feared the next step would be school uniforms. This cartoon is based on my mother's high school experience in the late 1960s—her principal made all the girls kneel on the floor as they came in each day to prove their skirts were knee-length or longer.

High school unpopularity makes ideal preparation for political cartooning. Not only did I write angry editorials for *The Review*, I was president of my high school's Rainbow Connection Gay/Straight Alliance. It may have been Massachusetts, but high school is high school, and the usual crop of ignoramuses took it upon themselves to bully our members and deface our posters with poorly-spelled slurs.

Another *Review* staff member took exception to "Stuck in the Middle Ages," a serious column I wrote about homophobia and gay teen suicide. His parody piece, "Stuck in the Doorways," attacked both gay and fat students and ran with a giant distorted photo of a belly. On a whim, I decided to respond with this "cartoon editorial."

The response was overwhelmingly positive, and I realized that most students had never bothered to read my original text-heavy column. If I wanted to be heard, cartooning was clearly the way to go!

In case you're wondering, our GSA was supported by the Safe Schools program started by (Republican) Governor William Weld—a program that his successor Mitt Romney later tried to destroy.

A big shout-out to the alumni of the Rainbow Connection, and all the teachers, administrators and students who supported us!

On a side note, you can see I used to wear many wordy thrift store T-shirts, ironic and otherwise.

I kept the angry cartoonist thing going my first year in college by drawing a few cartoons for *The Harvard Crimson*, though I didn't apply for a regular weekly slot until I was a senior. Can you tell I was a Women's Studies major?

Harvard's Republican Club actually had a Conservative Coming Out party where they served steak and apple pie and whined about how hard it was to be right-wing. Both on and off campus, conservative claims of being an oppressed minority got even louder once they controlled every branch of government.

Super-Bush really did rescue me—from a life of non-cartooning. I was so busy studying photography and anthropology, I put down my pen. And then came 9/11... and the Patriot Act, and the detention of innocent immigrants, and the bombing of Afghanistan and... I got a weekly slot in *The Crimson*, and haven't stopped since.

I may have mentioned that I've been a raving lunatic fan of Alison Bechdel since early high school. When I first got the guts a few years ago to write her a letter, she told me she particularly enjoyed this one and I nearly fainted from excitement. Goddamn Dubya's smirk, though. I can still barely watch him on the TV, it gets to me so bad.

I was talking in particular about Massachusetts, but this applies in general to the crazed emphasis on teaching to rigid standardized tests above all else, and throwing away any kids who fail to meet those standards.

There's nothing inherently good about tradition. Slavery and segregation were traditions. Second-class status for women was a tradition. If your tradition celebrates racist dirtwads, find a new damn tradition.

So-called "welfare reform" (thanks, Bill Clinton!) has everything to do with pushing abstinence until marriage, and nothing to do with narrowing the income gap. Its paper-thin premise is that poverty stems from promiscuous single mothers who stubbornly refuse to find someone to marry—and not from say, criminally low wages or lack of affordable childcare. But marriage doesn't magically make a minimum wage any less minimal, and single mothers often have good reason not to marry the fathers of their children, such as domestic violence.

For the first time in 351 years of sunny Harvard commencement ceremonies, it rained. I blame Bush.

And Sean Bell.

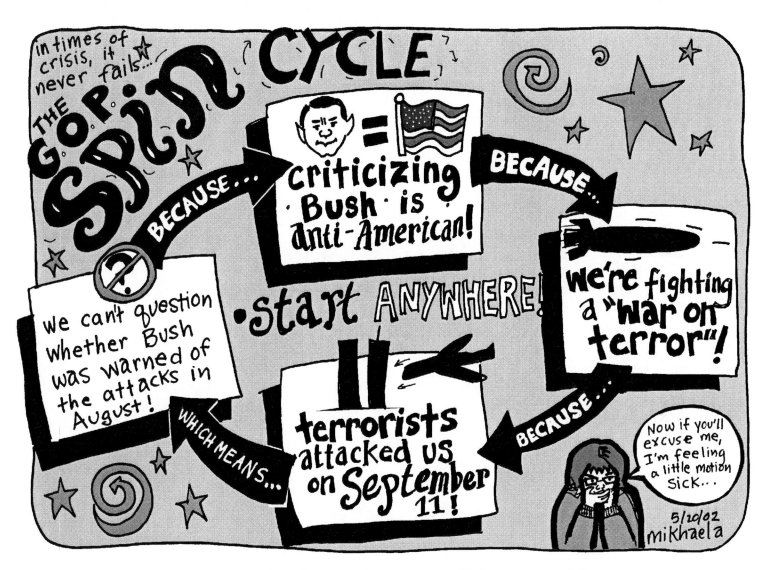

Remember when even Democrats wouldn't criticize Bush?

Regarding 9/11 tourism: I worked a few blocks from the World Trade Center site for three years, and I never got used to vendors hawking full color booklets of ghastly 9/11 photos ("Get your *Tragedy*, only five dollars! *Tragedy*, five dollars!"). It always puzzled me why people would want to take smiling family snapshots there, too.

The Supreme Court ruled 8-0 that public housing tenants could be evicted if a member of their household was using drugs, even if the tenant was unaware of the drug use and/or it occurred outside their home. *Nation* columnist Patricia Williams pointed out that Jeb Bush lived in public housing too—the Governor's mansion.

ABOUT THE CARTOONIST

MIKHAELA B. REID's cartoons have appeared in the *Los Angeles Times, The Guardian (UK), The Phoenix, Metro Times, Funny Times, Ms., Bitch, The Advocate, Girlfriends, Feministing.com, Chelsea Now, Campus Progress,* and assorted other fine publications and web sites.

Born in Lowell, Massachusetts, Reid graduated from Harvard University where she studied social anthropology and photography and drew weekly political cartoons for *The Harvard Crimson.* She has been a member of the Association of American Editorial Cartoonists since 2003 and is a founding member of Cartoonists with Attitude.

In 2004, Reid was featured as "cartooning's angry young woman" in the anthology *Attitude 2: The New Subversive Alternative Cartoonists,* edited by Ted Rall. In 2006, she was named one of Girls in Government's "Real Hot 100" and was featured in the Museum of Comics and Cartoon Art's exhibit "She Draws Comics: A Century of Women Cartoonists."

Reid lives in Brooklyn with fellow cartoonist Masheka Wood and their demented cat Riley. She blogs about cartooning and politics at **www.mikhaela.net**.